PROLOGUE

I could've easily lost faith in love this year. I learned that sometimes things don't pan out exactly how you dreamt it, and as much as you want it, as much love there is, sometimes it is not enough. In the process of accepting the loss of a love, I gained so much more in return. My outlook on love has been drastically touched and moved, it has transformed into something I never expected. I learned that love isn't something that can be chased, it's not an idea that you can create, plan, work, and execute. Love is not accepting potential as the foundation of your forever. Love isn't always a forever. Love sometimes can be a moment. Love isn't always another person. Love sometimes can just be you.

We often get fixated on the dreaminess of love and choose to ignore and accept that love is not a dream. It's real, it happens when we least expect it, it can come crashing down on you and like a wave quietly retrieve away, love isn't black and white, it's not always easy but it's also not hard at all. Love is not being the right choice, but being adamant in your choice because it's the only one that feels right, it's the only thing that makes sense even when it doesn't.

See, it wasn't until this year that I realized that as much as I call myself a hopeless romantic, I don't have a single clue what love is and it humbled me. It's okay to not know what it is, it's not made to be understood, it's not meant to be safe, it's not made, it just happens. You are only deserving of love if you are willing to say that you are not afraid, you don't want potential, you want the now and everything that comes with it. Love is meant to be felt, alone, together, in distance, in closeness, behind closed doors, in front of the world. Love is transcendental and the possibilities to it all are endless.

Love starts with you, allow yourself to get close to it, dare to be brave and fail, over and over again, because one day before you even notice the almost will finally be enough.

SOLIS OCCASUM

— What's with your obsession with sunsets?
I *think they're natures' answer to love. Sunsets are yours, but never to keep.*
— And how is that love? It's romantic to pine over something that'll never be yours? The cliche of unrequited love?
No. It's the acceptance of the fact that just because it's not yours you don't love it any less. You know it's not here to stay, yet - you wait for it to come around again.
Because everything you feel in that single moment is cosmic and when she leaves her beauty stays.
The feeling she gave you remains untouched by her absence.
Knowingly, you'll still find yourself anticipating her, even if it is just for a glimpse.
You'll keep moving forward, living your life, until you meet again in the infinite of her sunset.

AUREA HORA

just like the exact moment between the sunset and the moon rise,
it is not always visible but you can be sure without a doubt that it is there,
and will always be there, but to truly see it relies on the two most important things,
where you stand and the timing of it all

LONDON

clouds laid across her body like the finest silk
the rain made her skin glisten like diamonds
the city lights sparkled in her eyes, even the stars seemed
dimmed
and in between her curves I found myself lost
yet in every corner of her body I found something new to
explore
with every moment, sound, smell I found myself desiring more of
her unknown
I longed for something that I have never experienced before
and as the cold wrapped around me, I felt warm
unaware of its existence, it felt like home
she left me craving everything I had yet to taste
the uncertainty of something new yet it felt safe
sleepless nights to live in this everlasting dream
dreading the day I had to leave
but I left behind my wanderlust heart for her to keep
and in return she became the muse to my poetry

LOST&FOUND

years from now, I'll find you in my dreams
in every corner of my thoughts
in every inseam of my memories
you'll live in the words inspired by you
you'll exist in the vast of my heart
you'll be mine where it mattered the most
I'll be yours in our story untold

- something can't return, if it never left

12:27

There's some truth in our untold stories
Like when I struggled to hold onto your hand
as you danced and sung your way down the street after too many drinks
How you suddenly crashed into me in front of the Castro theatre
and with your eyes I became distracted long enough for you to steal a kiss
As I chased after you, I struggled to keep my feet on the ground and as I trailed behind you
I realized I would follow you until forever
Or maybe it was when we both lost our breath and felt onto the weak wired fence and smiled into each others faces
How you placed your head on my shoulder as we drove back home
and I was torn between what was more dangerous, keeping my eyes on you or missing out by keeping my eyes on the road?
And as I walked you to your door, I clutched your body in my arms, and you whispered what I never knew I was dying to hear
If I am being honest, there is some truth that lies in between some of these moments
Some of them happened, and some of them didn't
The reality to my fiction is that the words I never spoke were the most honest
and the things I wish I did were the loudest

TAM PROPE

drowning in the endless pit of possibilities never did me any good
in a way it was for me to make sense of things,
I thought the closure that I needed to pack it up and put it on the shelf
was subliminally in our texts so I analyzed them all,
or maybe it was somewhere on your couch so I recreated the moments in my head
If I could find what I did wrong,
or maybe what you did wrong
but as much as my mind was logical
my heart continued to be reckless
I grew tired, and my heart only ached as I tried to understand
maybe some things don't have an exact moment
maybe some things just don't make sense
maybe I was meant to fall in love
maybe I was meant to be heartbroken again
maybe, you, and I, were just meant to be close

so close yet so far

PROPTER TE

for everything that I was searching for
that I claimed I wanted
that I thought I couldn't reach
that I believed I deserved
you showed me that I could find it in me
that I had it all along
that it was already in my grasp
that I deserved so much more
for everything that I am not,
you showed me who I really am

CLOUDS

expectations dug into my shoulders and knotted my back
they made me believe that what I carried was the world
when in reality it was just stones in a bag to keep me in place
unable to move forward as it forced my head down
but one day, the weight felt a little lighter
the steps became easier to take
my shoulders cracked and the knots faded away
and as I looked behind I saw myself farther from where I was
all of the heavy scattered across the ground
and as I turned back around
my face was met by her hand
she cradled my chin with her thumb and index
tilting my head upwards by an inch
as my lungs filled with air
With nothing on my back but the wind now
I began to run, and just like that I started to fly
weightless and free, I was now among them
I could finally be me

DESIDERIUM

you wanted the moon, so I gave you the stars
you wanted the sea, so I gave you the breeze
you wanted it all, so I gave you me
it was not the moon
it was not the sea
it was not I, who made you lose sleep
but please,
keep all the stars
keep all the breeze
for when what you seek comes around
the big picture will be complete
and maybe then,
you know that I loved you unconditionally

11:11

this time comes around twice a day
the wish I make is always the same
and every time its made
it feels like a losing game
but today feels different
can you hold my heart if you're brave?
because all the wishes you make
all lead you back to my way
where I'd wish you stayed
but today feels different
and I hope you're not too late

SPACE

in the explosion of her galaxy
with every single kiss
she filled my empty abyss

AWAKE

sleeping turned into nightmares
when I didn't have you near
and even then
when you laid next to me asleep
I stayed awake
I knew the time I spent on earth
would only matter if it was spent
on you

MIXTAPE

everything was done intentionally
down to the title of the play-list
to the number of songs
to the lyrics themselves
hoping that the music would fill the gaps
of what was holding me back
maybe you skipped a track or two,
or never got around to playing it
maybe I expected you to listen to it thoroughly
then again
maybe everything was done too subliminally

WAITING

I stood there with every ounce of my body aching to kiss her
My hands screamed to caress her face to let her know how beautiful she was
My lips begged me to mouth her name and the five words that bounced in my head
My body yearned to have her warmth fill the cold skin that embraced the fire that burned for her
But, I wanted to kiss her with no traces of my broken soul
No crumbs of what my past love has left behind
No residue of the trauma my inner child carried
No remnants of who I was before
I wanted to press against her lips with courage, a healed heart, and more than anything
I wanted my kiss to tell her,
I'm not broken, but I'm not perfect,
I want you, but I don't need you,
I know you are worth it, but I will not lose my worth for it
I will never leave you, but I won't fix you,
I love you, but I will always love myself a little more

I stood there with every ounce of my body aching to kiss her,
but I'll endure the ache until my lips are ready to say...

DANCING

sometimes I run out of words to say
or I shy away from trying to explain
and when writers block is as its peak
I turn to my body to speak
because dancing for me
is another way to make poetry

MASTERPIECE

some took advantage of her naive heart
inflicting their empty shells they called souls on her gullible hope
but she chose to ignore and stood there gracefully
she embraced the world for what it was and could be
she accepted the ugly and called it beauty
mistreated and misunderstood,
underestimated and overlooked,
she took it and tore it apart,
to make something beautiful out of it
paint strokes of regret
colored lines of pain
the words of toxicity
ink of her love on the pen
acceptance fill the bucket of paint
sincerity behind her calligraphy
just like that,
a blank canvas was no more,
she framed it in gold
a masterpiece for you to hold

ALIS PROPRIIS VOLAT

daring for you to believe you can hold down my wings
its written in the stars, its spoken in my scars
your glass ceiling is calling me
to forge a new path with the shards
the boundaries of your expectations broken apart
in my eyes I hold the key
to fly and break free
love, it's up to you
are you brave enough for the leap?

DUM SPIRO SPERO

my knees trembled with every touch of a new bruise
my face carrying the scars of every fall
my hands ache in the clench of my callouses
but my lungs are relentless
as long as there is air to breath
I will drag, crawl, walk, or run
until I can hold the light of hope in my arms

EMPATHY

her smile was courageous and resilient
effortless and selfless
more for others than for herself
for she knew what it felt like to not have a single reason to do so
and she simply wanted nothing more
but to give someone a reason to

HOPELESSLY HOPEFUL

this year I experienced
endless winters in my soul
wet storms in my eyes
unbearable summers in my heart
but my spring has never bloomed this bright before
fields filled with the color of my optimism
humbled, I let go of everything I thought I knew
to rekindle the spark of curiosity for love
to set fire to my unwavering lust for life
as the seasons continued to cycle
and life continued to move
my beauty felt new every time
hopelessly hopeful for tomorrow
naive to think this is my prime
imagine what can happen in the fall

WORSHIP

like a devotee on a mission
her love was my religion
the scripture in the sound of her voice
the sounds we made like a choir in rejoice
god carefully crafted her features
making sure her lips were the preachers
her body the chapel, the gates of heaven beneath her waist
the eucharist on my tongue, it was how she taste

MIEL

con sus lentos besos y ojos oscuros
con sus labios tan dulce
y con su sabor de cajeta
me hace miel a tocar su piel

CRAZY

call me crazy
not because I want her
but because I think she wants me too
I know that she avoids the thought of me
how my name ricochets in her head late at night
when the noise of the day subsides
call me crazy
but the old me would've believed her lies
but I can see the truth now,
we both know you are mine
and as hard as you try, in the back of your head
you know you should be with me instead

EPIPHANY

she had nothing figured out,
yet she had it all
she wanted to create something out of nothing,
everything out of anything,
she had nothing figured out,
but she had all of me

ALIVE

Silly of me to think that love was calm and safe
Like the ocean breeze grazing your feet
as you stand close enough to the shore at the beach
But in fact,
its feeling weightless in the midst of an ocean in spite of the risk of drowning
its fighting to catch your breath as you free fall behind them
adrenaline rushing through your body as it prepares for impact
its falling in love with love herself,
not for what she was, or who she can be
It's standing in front of who she is, and all that it is,
and as I look at her in front of me,
My god,
I am not afraid anymore
I don't want to feel calm
I don't want to feel safe
I want to feel love
I want to feel alive

MARIPOSA

unexpectedly landing on my shoulder,
I recognize the rarity of it all,
a fleeting moment but it meant everything to me
I applied no pressure afraid to hurt its wings
accepted that it wasn't mine to keep
flighty creature,
always moving to the next best thing
in its absence, a clear awakening
it wasn't luck, it wasn't fate,
it was a choice that was made
even if the moment was gone
it thought I could be the one

TRUST

right now,
I am not the one you will sleep next to
I won't be sitting across from you while you eat dinner
the flowers at your door won't be from me
when that song plays I won't be dancing with you
your lips won't be the ones I kiss before I leave to work
the shoulder I rest my head on, on the flight isn't yours
the hand clutched in mine doesn't belong to you
maybe in this lifetime, maybe in the next one,
it'll finally be our turn
maybe today, maybe tomorrow
you can be mine, and I'll be yours
maybe I'll wait, maybe you'll hurry
but for right now,
I trust my heart enough to leave it up to fate
regardless, my feelings will remain the same
even if that's the only thing that's meant to be
trust me, it's the only thing that matters to me

ADVICE

they say those that give the best advice, never take it
you made me courageous, yet you're the most afraid
told me to love recklessly, fearlessly,
yet you're cautious, all the roads you take are all the same
afraid to experience the new unknown,
used to the same tricks of the game,
it always gets old, it's all you've ever known
bad at being in love, great with the pleasures,
maybe you do it for protective measures,
one day you'll take your own advice
and say what is showing in your eyes,
play it safe, keep loving me from a distance,
but I dare you to loosen up the resistance,
I am already at your side
what more do you need to hide?

ALWAYS

I always asked the same question
and always in return received the same answer
I never understood
and never content with their explanations
but now I finally know what they meant

So if you were to ask me the same question
I would give you the same answer
the one they would always give me
the one from back then

you just know

--- it's you

FIRST

our first kiss was like that exact moment when you reach
the peak of the highest rollercoaster of the park
our lips touched and my heart was no longer in my chest
but in my stomach instead

PHOTOSHOP

I hope when you photoshopped me out that pic
it helped you out a little bit
I'm okay if it did

POLAROIDS

not sure if we cropped it out too much
maybe we got it at the wrong angle
or the contrast was set too dark
or the saturation too high
some of them too blurry
others impossible to save with a filter
time and time again
you continued to try
to get our love to fit in a picture

TWO

my love is explicitly unbearable to hold
it's not meant for everyone
only understood for those who are bold
I don't have a doubt that you tried your best
my love, you are irreplaceable
and I must confess
I am sure that I will never love how I loved you again
but I promise that I won't give up on what I want
her love will be so powerful
that even when I know you're the one
she'd make me do what I thought would impossible
enough to make me love her in a way that I never loved you
she will make me realize that I will never love you any less
but she will show me that I can love so much more
putting my fears and regrets to rest,
and because of her I will be grateful that you and I met

grounded in your love, I will soar in her sky
you built my wings, but she will teach me how to fly

ALMOST

only I know my love is limitless
but then again,
maybe my past lovers know it too
because I know,
they spend eternal nights searching for it
even when they only got a glimpse of it
never even coming close to the infinite
but they keep trying and trying,
only to bury their void in an okay host
sad, that they'll always just come close
they'll have to settle with the almost

POSSIBLY

not sure if it's the choices I made or the ones made for me,
not sure if it's freedom or destiny,
not sure if it's in between yes or the maybe,
not sure if it's her and I, or you and me,
not sure if it's trusting the would be or the will be,
I can't be too sure of it all, surely,
but I am certain that being too sure is boring

INLOVE

in the absence of her love I discovered the presence of *love*
it was in the bottom of my coffee every morning
in gut clenching laughs shared between my friends and I
sometimes, only sometimes, I found it on my gym mat
in the afternoon over dinner with my family
between my thick blanket and my favorite show
I discovered it when I needed it the most
all along, it wasn't in an "us", or a "you"
I found it has, and will always be in me
and I can finally admit
that in the absence of love
love has always been present

FOR ME

every single question I shot at the sky
was met with silence echoing in the night
every scream and tear
wasted during the daylight
losses or lessons blurred in between
knocking me down to a plead
until it finally answered me
"like clay you are being shaped and molded
to the person you are meant to be
sometimes the clay will take a beating
but never leaving behind a bruise
in due time these doubts of yours will be through
and when the clay is perfected and set
it all wasn't done to you, but for you
for your potential to be met"

LIVE

sometimes I don't know what to do
but I act like I have a clue
told that having a plan is the only thing to make it right
but it's impossible to blueprint the way to live life
so here I am and here I stand with no plan
feeling great and doing the best that I can
time is a privilege and its all that you got
so with it, do it all and do all that you want

PROMISE

I wonder if your mind wanders back to the memories of us
what are we now but strangers with a mutual promise
where before my arms towered over you
finding safety in the exchanges of our secrets
where we shared little bits of us in songs
drawings and many letters filled our silences
my half of our matching bracelet sitting on my shelf
staring back at me every night
reminding me of how much I wish things weren't like this
how I miss competing over who had the smallest eyes
when each of us smiled
more than anything I just miss your smile
and although it's been a couple of years
I hope you know it's still alive more than ever
our promise, permanently resides in a place
where it only knows your name

SANDCASTLES

a forever is not an anchor
no such thing truly exists
its a word with no guarantee
created as a reminder that
time is not our friend and its indifferent
it doesn't care about how important it is
how much you cherish or value it
so don't use such an empty word
and hope that's all that it would take
because when the tide comes
your love is the only anchor
that will hold down the forte and
protect what matters the most

YOU UP?

Why do you only meet me in the closet?
Get upset with me when I want to stop it?
telling others that it's just for fun and pretend
yet your name always pops up after ten?
if you're going to leave then close the door
and don't keep it open for me when you're bored
next time, let's meet in the daylight
unless you're afraid I'll realize
that you're nothing but another night?
and I am just something you want to try?

TELL ME

I wonder what made it so easy to say
but so difficult to stay?

LET ME

please let me let you go
I know I am doing better on my own
because needing me is not wanting me
and my arms are not a shelter
for you to come and go
my heart can't bare the ins and outs
it was never meant to be for rent
and it should never be returned
I'll admit, I am in love
but I've accepted that there's so much to me
than being with you
love shouldn't be my everything
but it can be the only thing
that keeps me moving forward
because if beings yours
takes me from me
if I am an option and not a choice
I rather be alone
because I know I'm the right one
but its not my responsibility
to prove it to you
that's something you should already know
so with every word and every turned page
I hope you know
I am letting you go

UNTITLED

I wrote to immortalize you
every word breathing life back into you
but my words have ran out of life to give
with every flick of my pen the thought of you escapes
every written poem is now titled and dated
and with the turning of the pages
my words are laying you to rest in my head
the word us is disassociating with the word you
and as your book will lie on my shelf
as my most prize possession
the chapters that started it all
are finally closing where
no bookmark is to be found
like any great writer knows
that a new chapter must follow
because a new book awaits
yearning to be written
and I am finally ready to write it

LATE-NIGHT DRIVE

we went from having it all
now all we have is missed calls
we went from memories in a car
now all we have is driving us apart

MOVING

I gathered my thoughts on the way out of your heart
in the midst of packing it all up and throwing some things away
the realization hit me like a moving truck
you fell out of love with me, you say
because I wasn't the same person I was before
I propelled forward while you were stuck in reverse
your love was not enough to bind who I was yet to become
so if my growth made you uneasy and uncomfortable
I don't have an apology waiting for you
you should've known that with my changes
 I never loved you any less
In fact, I continued to grow alongside the love I had for you
but I guess for you that wasn't enough
so with a full heart and a slight idea of who I am
I decided to walk away and your resentment made you blind
to see the foot prints I left for you in the sand

SIX

I walked to the edge of the shore and began to scream
in hopes of having every thought of you claw itself out of my throat
ripped and tore apart the pieces of you until it effortlessly slipped through my fingers
and every tear wiped away every kiss, touch and dream that we shared
the pain and the hurt made me realize that I failed to see
that what was truly flying out my throat was the butterflies I had for you before
the ones that would flourish every time I mentioned your name and a smile would follow
and what was slipping through my fingers where the remaining ashes of the walls you broke down
every kiss, touch, and dream that we shared polished and cleansed by each tear
and through this all I failed to remember that you always had that effect on me
motivating me to always be the best version of me that I could be
because while loving you made me incredible
it was losing you that made me invincible
because my throat will heal and speak something new
my hands have grown stronger and learned to rebuild
and when I think of you and shed a tear
it will be a reminder of the best years

LOS ANGELES

we run to the city of angels with suitcases filled with demons
etching our names on the walls of abandoned buildings
searching for our dreams in the Hollywood streets
sitting at the edge of expensive rooftops risking our life
for our fingertips to simply graze those we envy in the sky
but when the luxury wool curtains close and lay fame to sleep
all the streets start to all look the same
movie like replicas of what we originally tried to escape

SUNLIGHT

the "it's okay, everything will be alright"
the compass you use as a guide
the north star in the night
the reason to stay alive
she's your sunlight

--the flower can't bloom without the sun

REMINDER

there is over 7.8 billion people in the world
but only one of you
only one version of your smile
your laugh, your hug, your love,
only one version of all that you are
if that doesn't make you exceptionally more than enough
I'll spend every 1,440 minutes of 365 days
to remind you
that you are not only 1 in a million
but 1 in a lifetime

SUPERPOWERS

I can't fly nor
do I have super strength
I can't see through walls nor
can I run at the speed of light
but every time I fall
I get up every time

CONFIDENCE

if my mirror could speak she would tell you
that I stare at myself every morning
repeating the same words over and over again
and she felt so special to receive such high compliments
but then she would tell you that she would be confused
when the same words would be used when I stared at her
with eyes filled with sorrow and fear
and then the compliments didn't feel so good
but the more it happened the more she realized
that the words I said weren't for her
but for me instead

NOTICE

Dear friend,

it's been a long time since we spoke and I am concerned
you haven't been yourself as of late
I hope you know that it's okay to not be okay
you don't always have to fake a smile
and pretend that everything is alright
so even when you can't make me laugh
or look me in the eye
I am your friend, unconditionally
so if you're going to be sad, feel safe enough
to do it with me

Please,

the letter that I needed

CONTROL

insecurities holding me on pause
regrets placing me in reverse
fearing falling back
but now here I am
insecurities turning off
regrets being muted
fearlessly falling forward

WHO

I am still naive as if I was fifteen
still trying to make sense of things
I am still curious as if I was five
understanding what it is to be alive
I am still clueless as if I was a newborn
wondering why I was even born
I am twenty-four years old
but truth be told
I am just starting to figure out
what I want and what matters the most
I hope by forty I know who I am
if not, it'll be fun to see what more to this poem I can add

NOW

tomorrow is something that can't exist without the now
and now wouldn't be what it is without yesterday
so take it slow
and take it day by day
and be proud of yourself
for how far you've come today
live passionately in the moment with no fear
because once its done nothing will be the same
against the clock, we'll always lose to time
so let's live to the fullest and never lose in vain

TOMORROW

tomorrow always brings a new opportunity
a new beginning and a new possibility
because truthfully,
a new almost is always closer than it seems

REASON

I have to be honest with myself and most importantly honest with you.
It's more than difficult to tap into everything we've been through and accumulate enough content to formulate a poem, or even a proper sentence because I selfishly don't want to share you with the world just yet. Because at least in everything that you've inspired, you are still mine and everything is still pure and rich filled with all that you are and all that we were. I could spend eternal lifetimes writing about every single thing you have made me feel and even then it wouldn't suffice or justify the love I have embedded in my soul for you. Unspoken poems reside in hidden places for me to make sure a small part of you will remain untouched and untainted. With time that love will transform because all everlasting things do to make sure they are not forgotten and can withstand any changes. Your love was the reason behind my smile for many years, and even now it will continue to be, because when I think of you that's all that I can do.

-- my brown eyed blues will sparkle from a distance knowing that loving you was my biggest privilege.

I used to be afraid of sharing my most intimate moments with the world, thinking it would provide others the opportunity to abuse my vulnerability. But in the process of writing this book I have found strength in my discomfort and in return I have been able to heal, release and build the courage to keep moving forward with my heart on my sleeve open to life itself and all that it brings.

If you are reading this, I can't thank you enough. This is only the beginning and I can't wait for the possibilities to unravel itself in front of us together on this journey.

With love,
@thejys

CSP180874-1
The responsible publisher is jys.

www.ingramcontent.com/pod-product-compliance
Lightning Source LLC
Chambersburg PA
CBHW061344040426
42444CB00011B/3072